ANIMAL WRANGLER

WILD JOBS

LAURA K. MURRAY

CREATIVE EDUCATION · CREATIVE PAPERBACKS

PUBLISHED BY CREATIVE EDUCATION AND CREATIVE PAPERBACKS
P.O. Box 227, Mankato, Minnesota 56002
Creative Education and Creative Paperbacks are
imprints of The Creative Company
www.thecreativecompany.us

DESIGN AND PRODUCTION by Joe Kahnke
Art direction by Rita Marshall
Printed in the United States of America

PHOTOGRAPHS by Alamy (13UG 13th, AF archive, FORRAY Didier/
SAGAPHOTO.COM, ITAR-TASS Photo Agency, Grega Rozac, United
Archives GmbH, ZUMA Press, Inc.), Getty Images (David Caird/Newspix,
Ryan McVay), iStockphoto (evemilla, paylessimages), LostandTaken.com,
Shutterstock (Stanislav Duben, Emmeewhite, fivespots, Husjak, Petrovic
Igor, Anan Kaewkhammul, Seth LaGrange, Betti Luna, Nik Merkulov,
Miloje, mountainpix, pattyphotoart, Aleksey Stemmer, Tooykrub)

Library of Congress Cataloging-in-Publication Data
Names: Murray, Laura K., author.
Title: Animal wrangler / Laura K. Murray.
Series: Wild Jobs.
Includes bibliographical references and index.
Summary: A brief exploration of what animal wranglers do on the job,
including the equipment they use and the training they need, plus real-
life instances of animal wrangling on movie sets such as the Harry Potter
series.
Identifiers: ISBN 978-1-60818-921-2 (hardcover) / ISBN 978-1-62832-
537-9 (pbk) / ISBN 978-1-56660-973-9 (eBook)
This title has been submitted for CIP processing under LCCN 2017940118.

CCSS: RI.1.1, 2, 3, 4, 5, 6, 7; RI.2.1, 2, 4, 5, 6; RI.3.1, 2, 5, 7; RF.1.1, 3, 4; RF.2.3, 4

FIRST EDITION HC 9 8 7 6 5 4 3 2 1
FIRST EDITION PBK 9 8 7 6 5 4 3 2 1

CONTENTS

CAMERAS ARE ROLLING ON THE SET.

The grizzly bear's dark eyes shine. It stands up on its hind legs. The bear's paws are heavy on your shoulders. You have trained to wrestle each other!

1 WILD WORK

An animal wrangler trains and cares for animals. The wrangler works with animals in movies, TV shows, commercials, and music videos.

Wranglers work with animals as
big as elephants or as small as ants.

They work with everything from clucking chickens to hissing snakes.

2
TRAINING WITH CARE

Wranglers may keep animals on a ranch, farm, or zoo. They train the animals to perform. Then the wranglers move the animals to a film set. They work with the actors and crew.

Every set is different. There might be **SPECIAL EFFECTS** like loud explosions. The wrangler keeps the animal calm and safe. The animal needs water, food, shade, and shelter. It needs breaks, too.

3
LEARNING ON THE JOB

Animal wranglers may get special training **CERTIFICATIONS**. Some wranglers take science classes about animal behavior. Others learn to do **STUNTS**. They find out how to control the animals. They use collars, leashes, muzzles, lasers, or other equipment.

FALCONRY GLOVE

Animal wranglers may wear padding, gloves, or special sleeves for protection. They carry nets or shields. They have fire extinguishers, too. They keep **ANTIDOTE** for **VENOMOUS** animals.

4 WIZARDING ANIMALS

Animal wranglers worked on the Harry Potter movie sets. They trained dogs, cats, and rats. Owls were the most difficult to train. An owl named Gizmo played Hedwig in two films.

5 IS WRANGLING FOR YOU?

Animal wranglers keep animals safe and ready to perform. Would *you* want to be an animal wrangler when you grow up?

YOU BE THE ANIMAL WRANGLER!

Imagine you are an animal wrangler. Read the questions below about your wild job. Then write your answers on a separate sheet of paper. Draw a picture of yourself as an animal wrangler!

My name is ———. I am an animal wrangler.

1. What is your favorite animal to work with?
2. What does the skin of a snake feel like? How about the fur of a tiger?
3. What noises do your animals make?
4. What sorts of equipment do you need?
5. How do you keep your animals safe?

GLOSSARY

ANTIDOTE: a medicine to stop the effects of a poison

CERTIFICATIONS: proofs of certain skills

SET: the place where a movie or show is filmed

SPECIAL EFFECTS: images or sounds made for a movie or show, often using computers, props, or cameras

STUNTS: tricks or skilled actions in a movie or show

VENOMOUS: able to inject a poison called venom by fangs, stingers, or other body parts

READ MORE

Loh-Hagan, Virginia. *Big Animal Trainer*.
Ann Arbor, Mich.: Cherry Lake, 2017.

Perish, Patrick. *Animal Trainer*.
Minneapolis: Bellwether Media, 2015.

WEBSITES

Animal Info
https://seaworld.org/en/animal-info/
Learn more about working with animals.

Animal Magic
*http://www.scholastic.com/browse/article
.jsp?id=5802*
Read an interview with an animal wrangler who
worked on the Harry Potter movies.

Note: Every effort has been made to ensure that the websites listed above are suitable for children, that they have educational value, and that they contain no inappropriate material. However, because of the nature of the Internet, it is impossible to guarantee that these sites will remain active indefinitely or that their contents will not be altered.

INDEX